Ready-to-Use
Independent Reading
Management Kit
Grades 4-6

by Beverley Jones and Maureen Lodge

SCHOLASTIC
PROFESSIONAL BOOKS

New York ■ Toronto ■ London ■ Auckland ■ Sydney ■ Mexico City ■ New Delhi ■ Hong Kong ■ Buenos Aires

Dedication

We would like to thank all teachers who share their ideas and expertise. We especially want to thank Stacie Martino and Arla Pickens for their contribution to this book.

Beverley Jones
Maureen Lodge

Scholastic Inc. grants teachers permission to photocopy the reproducible pages from this book for classroom use. No other part of this publication may be reproduced in whole or in part, or stored in a retrieval system, or transmitted in any form or by any means, electronic, mechanical, photocopying, recording, or otherwise, without written permission of the publisher. For information regarding permission, write to Scholastic Inc., 557 Broadway, New York, NY 10012.

Cover design by Frank Maiocco

Cover photograph © Ken O'Donoghue/S.O.D.A.

Interior design by Ellen Matlach Hassell
for Boultinghouse & Boultinghouse

Cover and interior illustrations by Mick Reid

ISBN: 0-439-36591-0

Contents

Introduction

The *Ready-to-Use Independent Reading Management Kit: Grades 4–6* was born out of the need for reading and writing activities that meet the diverse levels of learners in the classroom. Our solution was to develop independent reading contracts, which are a series of activity packs that can be used with any book and a variety of genres.

For each contract, students make choices about which reading, writing, and skill-building activities they will complete. Making choices fosters a sense of responsibility and ownership, which encourages students to take the contract seriously. This program helps students learn to select appropriate books, organize the materials they need, and work independently on meaningful and structured activities that help them get the most out of their reading experiences. The program also allows teachers to work with one group of students while the rest of the class works independently on their contracts.

The ten different contracts in this book are designed to be used with books of various genres. There are five contracts for general fiction, and one contract each for biography, mystery, realistic fiction, adventure, and nonfiction. The contracts can be used in any order. Each contract is organized into four categories: reading, writing, skills, and art. Within the skills category, you'll find activities relating to parts of speech, spelling, vocabulary, and more. Many activities are accompanied by appealing, illustrated reproducible sheets to help kids stay on task. Students will write an advice column for a character, create a setting slide show, write character fortune cookies, play a game about verbs and adverbs, and much, much more!

The variety of activities within each contract and the flexibility to use the contracts with any book will help you meet the needs of all your learners. The section titled How to Use This Book on pages 6–8 will take you through the process step by step, from helping students learn to select books to assessing their work. At the end of the book, you'll find other useful reproducible materials, including a letter home explaining the program, a blank contract, assessment rubrics, and more. We think you'll find these independent reading contracts to be a valuable tool for enriching reading, writing, and language arts. Happy reading!

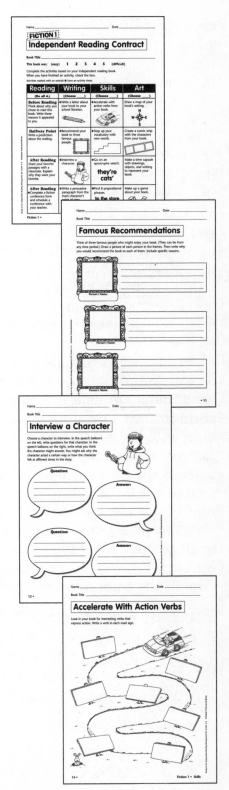

How to Use This Book

Setting Up the System

To meet the needs of all students, collect books that represent a wide range of reading levels. These books can be from your own collection, the school or public library, or donations from families.

Store the books by level in boxes or on shelves, to help students make selections more easily. We have found it helpful to stock a center with books, independent reading contracts, copies of the activity pages, and any necessary supplies. To help students work independently, show them where everything is kept and how to put away materials when they have finished using them.

At the top of the writing, skills, and art columns on each contract, you'll find a space to fill in the number of activities you wish students to complete in each category. This can be determined by the amount of time you want to spend on each contract or by the particular area you want to focus on. It also presents an opportunity to modify the assignment for individual students, if necessary. After filling in the number of activities for each column, make a copy of the contract for each student.

In advance, determine how long you would like students to spend on each contract. We have found that two to three weeks is usually a good amount of time. Although students work at different rates, it's possible to set a time frame within which all children can work.

If a student finishes a contract for one book, he or she can complete an additional contract in the same genre for a new book if time permits. Set aside a few blocks of time each week for children to work on their contracts. Once students are comfortable with the procedures, they can work independently while you meet with individuals or small groups. This is also a good time to have conferences with students who have completed a contract. (See Completing a Contract, page 8.)

Student Selection of Literature

To introduce independent reading contracts in your classroom, begin by demonstrating how to choose a book that is just right for the reader. For example, you might pose these questions for children to use:

- What is this book about?

- Does the subject interest me?

- Can I read the book without much difficulty?

By showing books that are too easy, too difficult, and just right, you can set an example of appropriate book selection.

Introducing New Skills

Before introducing an independent reading contract, look it over to note the skills that children need to complete it. For instance, before beginning the Mystery contract, children need to know about conjunctions and interrogatives. One or two weeks before introducing the contract, conduct mini-lessons to introduce the skill. Students will then practice that skill as they complete the contract.

When introducing terms such as adjectives, proper nouns, or homophones, you may want to make a poster with examples of these words on it. Students can then refer to the poster if their book does not offer a wide variety of these types of words. In our classroom, students have also enjoyed adding to the posters as they come across "poster words" in their books.

Starting an Independent Reading Contract

Once students have selected their books, model how to use an independent reading contract for a book the whole class has read. Make an overhead transparency of a contract sheet. After students have finished reading the book, show them the contract. Fill in the name, date, and book title lines, and circle the reading level from 1 to 5. Explain that each student will fill in this information and complete the activities based on his or her own independent reading book.

Point out that the first column on the contract lists reading activities. Students should complete all activities in this column, beginning with the first. The activities specify when students should complete them: before reading, at the halfway point, and after reading.

Explain that as students complete each activity, they should make a check mark in the corresponding square on the contract. Explain that after children complete the reading activities, they can do the activities in the other columns in any order they wish. Also, point out the number of activities per column that students should complete.

Draw students' attention to the asterisk in the corner of the boxes on the contract and explain that this means there is a reproducible page on which to complete the activity. Show students where they can find these activity pages. It is helpful to keep the activity pages for each contract in a labeled folder. Demonstrate the procedures students should follow for activities that do not have reproducible sheets.

Show students where to find materials, as well as how to use them and put them away. For example, students will need basic art supplies for many of the activities in the art column. You may want to set up an art center for this purpose. (If you are short on art supplies, you might send home a letter to families with a wish list of supplies.)

Storing Work in Progress

Completing an independent reading contract may take a couple of weeks. It is important to help students organize their materials so that they can work effectively on their own. Have students store all of their materials for their current contract in a pocket folder, including their book. It is helpful for students to staple their contract to the inside left of their folder for easy reference. Designate a place for students to keep their folders, such as in their desks or in a file folder box.

Meeting the Needs of Your Students

There are a variety of ways to use independent reading contracts to meet your students' range of needs. Contracts can be used with books of any reading level. We have found that it works best to have all students work on the same contract at the same time. The reading level of the books that students choose and the number of books they read tailor the program to meet each student's needs.

We set aside a three-week period for students to work on each contract. During this time, one student may complete activities for one book while another student may complete activities for three books. Use the blank independent reading contract on page 126 to create additional contracts that reflect skills you would like to reinforce.

Completing a Contract

Once a student has completed an independent reading contract, he or she should fill out a self-assessment rubric (page 122). You may wish to model this procedure by evaluating sample work that you have created. Then the student prepares for a teacher conference by completing the appropriate conference form (pages 114–119) and scheduling a conference with you. Now that the student is ready to "check out" he or she fills out a checkout form (page 121) to make sure that all work has been completed. Have students staple their work in order, along with the contract, the self-assessment rubric, the conference form, and the checkout form on top. Students should put all of this into a folder and turn in their work at a designated spot. (This could be a basket on your desk or a file folder box in a reading center.) During conferences, you can help students evaluate their work. An additional assessment form for you to evaluate students' work appears on page 123. You can also keep a record of each student's work throughout the year by using the reproducible Teacher Record on page 124.

New Contracts

Once students have mastered the skills on a contract, they are ready to progress to a new contract. We recommend discussing and modeling the use of each contract as you introduce it. This is also a good opportunity to discuss any issues that arise about procedures, materials, behavior, and performance. Throughout the year, continue to model procedures to reinforce and ensure the quality of both the work and the working environment.

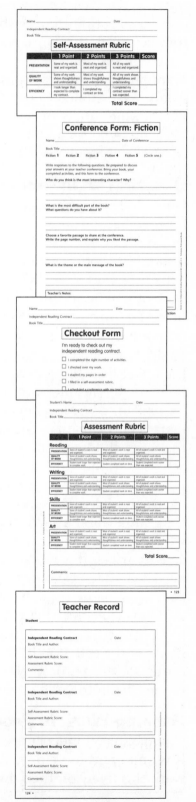

Name _____ Date _____

FICTION 1
Independent Reading Contract

Book Title _____

This book was: (easy) **1   2   3   4   5**   (difficult)

Complete the activities based on your independent reading book.
When you have finished an activity, check the box.

Activities marked with an asterisk ✱ have an activity sheet.

Reading	Writing	Skills	Art
(Do all 4.)	**(Choose ____)**	**(Choose ____)**	**(Choose ____)**
Before Reading Think about why you chose to read this book. Write three reasons it appealed to you.	✱Write a letter about your book to your school librarian.	✱Accelerate with action verbs from your book.	Draw a map of your book's setting.
Halfway Point Write a prediction about the ending.	✱Recommend your book to three famous people.	✱Step up your vocabulary with new words.	Create a comic strip with the characters from your book.
After Reading Share your favorite passages with a classmate. Explain why they were your favorite.	✱Interview a character.	✱Go on an apostrophe search. they're cats'	Make a time capsule with drawings, objects, and writing to represent your book.
After Reading ✱Complete a fiction conference form and schedule a conference with your teacher.	✱Write a persuasive paragraph from a character's point of view.	✱Find 8 prepositional phrases. to the store up the tree	Make up a game about your book.

Ready-to-Use Independent Reading Management Kit: Grades 4–6   Scholastic Professional Books

Name_____ Date _____

Book Title _____

Letter to a Librarian

Write a letter to your school or local librarian. Explain why a librarian should or should not recommend this book. Include specific details about the book and why students your age would or would not like to read it.

Ready-to-Use Independent Reading Management Kit: Grades 4–6   Scholastic Professional Books

Name _____ Date _____

Book Title _____

Famous Recommendations

Think of three famous people who might enjoy your book. (They can be from
any time period.) Draw a picture of each person in the frames. Then write why
you would recommend the book to each of them. Include specific reasons.

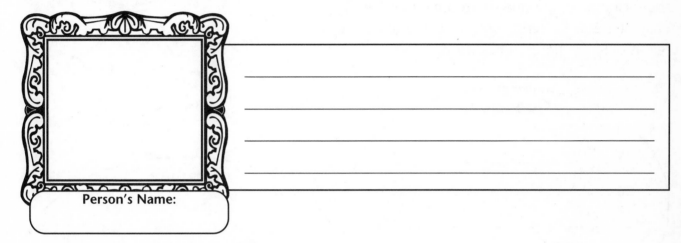

Person's Name:

Person's Name:

Person's Name:

Name_____ Date _____

Book Title _____

Interview a Character

Choose a character to interview. In the speech balloons on the left, write questions for that character. In the speech balloons on the right, write what you think the character might answer. You might ask why the character acted a certain way or how the character felt at different times in the story.

Question:
_____
_____
_____

Answer:
_____
_____
_____

Question:
_____
_____
_____

Answer:
_____
_____
_____

Ready-to-Use Independent Reading Management Kit: Grades 4–6 Scholastic Professional Books

Persuasive Paragraph

Think of a point in the story at which a character would like to persuade someone to do something. Write a persuasive paragraph from that character's point of view. Include convincing arguments the character might give.

Character _____

_____

_____

_____

_____

_____

_____

_____

_____

_____

_____

_____

_____

_____

_____

_____

_____

_____

Accelerate With Action Verbs

Look in your book for interesting verbs that
express action. Write a verb in each road sign.

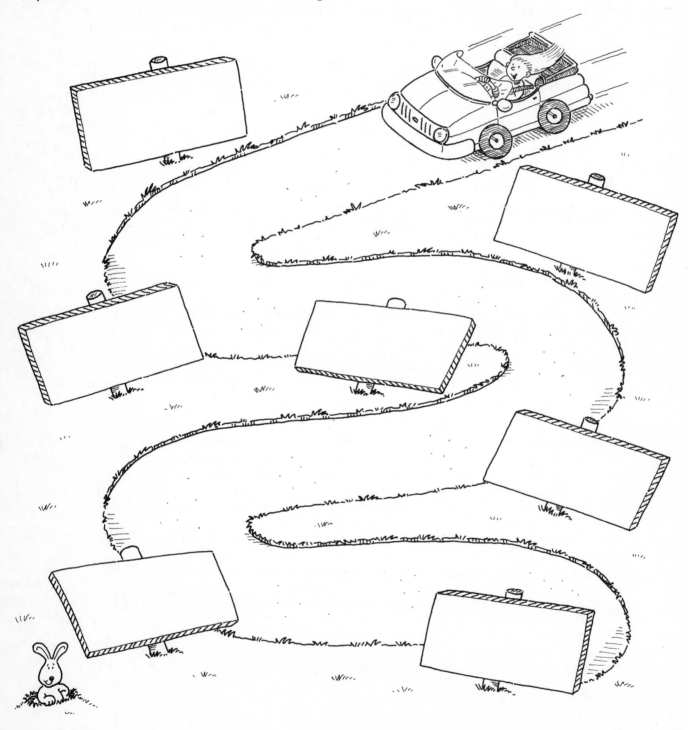

Ready-to-Use Independent Reading Management Kit: Grades 4–6   Scholastic Professional Books

Name _____ Date _____

Book Title _____

Step Up Your Vocabulary!

Find two new words in your book. Fill in the information in each box. You may fill in more than one sheet to step up your vocabulary even more!

Your own sentence that uses the word

Sentence from your book that uses the word

Synonym(s)

Definition

Word

Your own sentence that uses the word

Sentence from your book that uses the word

Synonym(s)

Definition

Word

Ready-to-Use Independent Reading Management Kit: Grades 4–6   Scholastic Professional Books

Name _____ Date _____

Book Title _____

Apostrophe Search

Apostrophes can be used in contractions.

EXAMPLES: **it's = it is**   **they're = they are**

Apostrophes can also be used to show possession.

EXAMPLES: **Brendan's bicycle   cats' tails**

Look in your book for words with apostrophes. Write them in the appropriate column. If the apostrophe shows possession, also write the object that is owned.

Contractions	Possession
you're	Jen's desk

Ready-to-Use Independent Reading Management Kit: Grades 4–6   Scholastic Professional Books

Name_____ Date _____

Book Title _____

Prepositional Phrases

A prepositional phrase includes a preposition
and the object of the preposition.

I walk to school.

PREPOSITION = to

OBJECT OF THE PREPOSITION = school

Bowser barked at the mail carrier.

PREPOSITION = at

OBJECT OF THE PREPOSITION = mail carrier

Copy eight sentences from your book that include prepositional phrases.
Circle each preposition and underline its object.

1. _____

2. _____

3. _____

4. _____

5. _____

6. _____

7. _____

8. _____

Ready-to-Use Independent Reading Management Kit: Grades 4–6   Scholastic Professional Books

Name_____ Date_____

FICTION 2
Independent Reading Contract

Book Title _____

This book was: (easy)   **1   2   3   4   5**   (difficult)

Complete the activities based on your independent reading book.
When you have finished an activity, check the box.

Activities marked with an asterisk ✱ have an activity sheet.

Reading	Writing	Skills	Art
(Do all 4.)	**(Choose ____)**	**(Choose ____)**	**(Choose ____)**
Before Reading ✱Make a vocabulary-building bookmark.	✱Write a setting postcard.	✱Fill in the double-vision verb sheet with *-ing* verbs.	✱Design a CD cover. Think of song titles that relate to your book.
Halfway Point Find an interesting dialogue between two characters. Ask a classmate to join you in reading it aloud, like a script.	✱Make a character wish list.	✱Find awesome adverbs in your book. **gently**	Imagine that your class is putting on a play based on your book. Make a poster to advertise the play.
After Reading Write and study the definitions of your bookmark words. Ask a classmate to quiz you on them.	✱Write a news article. **Who? What? When? Why? Where?**	✱Create a vocabulary scramble and challenge a classmate to solve it. **CRESBLAM**	Look in magazines for pictures of people that remind you of characters from your book. Make a collage and write the characters' names.
After Reading ✱Complete a fiction conference form and schedule a conference with your teacher.	✱Compose a shaped poem. *A clock keeping time, my heart beats constantly, counting out the hours and days and weeks and years of my life. Tick, tock, thump, thump.*	✱Play Proper Noun Concentration. proper noun _Serena_ common noun _girl_	Draw or paint an abstract or realistic picture that represents the theme of the book. Write a title that relates to the theme.

Ready-to-Use Independent Reading Management Kit: Grades 4–6   Scholastic Professional Books

Name _____ Date _____

Book Title _____

Vocabulary-Building Bookmark

Write the title of your book and draw a picture. Cut out the bookmark. As you read your book, write new words on the lines.

Book Title _____

_____

_____

_____

_____

_____

_____

_____

_____

_____

_____

_____

_____

_____

_____

_____

_____

Name _____ Date _____

Book Title _____

Write a Setting Postcard

Imagine that you are visiting an important setting in the story. Write a postcard to a friend, describing the place. Describe what it looks like and what there is to do there. Cut out the postcard and draw a picture of the setting on the back.

Fiction 2 • Writing

Character Wish List

Make a list of objects the main character might like to own. Think about that character's goals and what would help him or her achieve those goals. Also consider what your character likes to do. Beside each object, write a brief explanation of why the character would want it. Write as if you were the character.

My Wish List

by _____
Character's Name

_____ _____

_____ _____

_____ _____

_____ _____

_____ _____

_____ _____

_____ _____

Noteworthy News Article

The climax is the most exciting part of a story. It tells how the conflict or problem is resolved. Write an article for a newspaper, describing the climax of your book. Draw a picture and write a caption beneath it. Answer the questions below.

1. Who? _____

_____

_____

2. What? _____

_____

_____

3. When? _____

_____

4. Where? _____

_____

_____

5. Why was this event so important?

_____

_____

_____

Shaped Poem

A shaped poem (also known as a concrete or picture poem) forms a simple picture of its subject—for example, a poem about a heart would form a heart shape. Think of an important object or creature in your book and write a poem about it in the space below. On a separate sheet of unlined paper, lightly draw a simple outline of the object or creature. Then, copy your poem along the lines of the drawing.

my heart beats constantly, counting out the hours and days and weeks and years of my life. Thump, thump. Like a clock keeping time, Tick, tock, thump, thump, thump, thump

_____

_____

_____

_____

_____

_____

_____

_____

_____

_____

_____

_____

_____

_____

_____

_____

_____

_____

Double-Vision Verbs

If a verb has one syllable, has a short-vowel sound, and ends in a single consonant, then double the final consonant before adding *-ing*.

Look in your book for verbs that require you to double the final consonant when adding *-ing*. Fill in the eyeglasses below. Write the verb on the left side and the verb plus *-ing* on the right side.

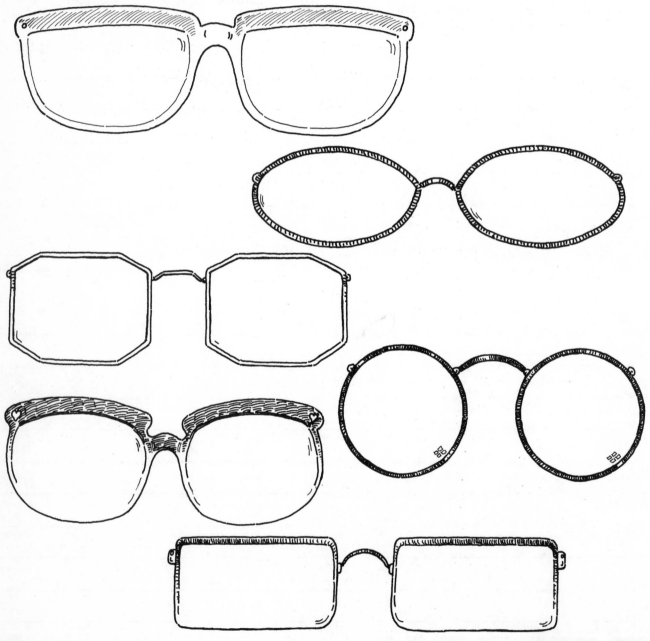

Ready-to-Use Independent Reading Management Kit: Grades 4–6 Scholastic Professional Books

Fiction 2 • Skills

Awesome Adverbs

An adverb is a word that describes a verb. Look in your book for interesting adverbs and write them in the left-hand column. Then write a sentence using each adverb. Draw an arrow from the adverb to the verb it describes. The first one has been done for you.

Adverb   Sentence

1. ___gently___   The snow fell gently throughout the night.

2. _____   _____

3. _____   _____

4. _____   _____

5. _____   _____

6. _____   _____

7. _____   _____

8. _____   _____

9. _____   _____

10. _____   _____

Vocabulary Scramble

Make a vocabulary scramble! First look in your book for new vocabulary words. (They should have nine letters or fewer so that they will fit in the boxes below.) Look up each word in the dictionary and write the definition as a clue. Then scramble the order of the letters in each word and write them in the boxes. Write the answers at the bottom of the page, then fold along the line to hide the answers. Challenge a classmate to unscramble the words.

EXAMPLE: | A | R | B | S | L | E | M | C | Write a letter in each box.

Clue: _to mix up_____

Word: SCRAMBLE_____

1. ⬜⬜⬜⬜⬜⬜⬜⬜

Clue: _____

_____

Word: _____

2. ⬜⬜⬜⬜⬜⬜⬜

Clue: _____

_____

Word: _____

3. ⬜⬜⬜⬜⬜⬜

Clue: _____

_____

Word: _____

4. ⬜⬜⬜⬜⬜⬜⬜⬜⬜

Clue: _____

_____

Word: _____

5. ⬜⬜⬜⬜⬜⬜⬜⬜

Clue: _____

_____

Word: _____

6. ⬜⬜⬜⬜⬜⬜⬜

Clue: _____

_____

Word: _____

Answers: 1. _____ **3.** _____ **5.** _____

2. _____ **4.** _____ **6.** _____

Ready-to-Use Independent Reading Management Kit: Grades 4–6   Scholastic Professional Books

Fiction 2 • Skills

Proper Noun Concentration

A proper noun names a particular person, place, or thing. It's easy to spot proper nouns because they are capitalized. Look in your book for proper nouns. Write each proper noun in a box. In the box next to it, write the appropriate common noun. When you are finished, cut out the boxes, place them facedown, and play Concentration. Try to find matching pairs of proper and common nouns.

proper noun	common noun	proper noun	common noun
Serena	girl	Sylvester	cat
proper noun	common noun	proper noun	common noun
Texas	state		
proper noun	common noun	proper noun	common noun
proper noun	common noun	proper noun	common noun
proper noun	common noun	proper noun	common noun
proper noun	common noun	proper noun	common noun
proper noun	common noun	proper noun	common noun
proper noun	common noun	proper noun	common noun

Name_____ Date _____

Book Title _____

CD Cover

Imagine that a band has made a CD of songs that are about your book. Design a CD cover that represents the book. On the lines, write song titles that relate to the book.

Song Titles:

_____ _____

_____ _____

_____ _____

_____ _____

Ready-to-Use Independent Reading Management Kit: Grades 4–6 Scholastic Professional Books

Name_____ Date_____

Independent Reading Contract

Book Title _____

This book was: (easy) **1   2   3   4   5** (difficult)

Complete the activities based on your independent reading book.
When you have finished an activity, check the box.

Activities marked with an asterisk ✱ have an activity sheet.

Reading	Writing	Skills	Art
(Do all 4.)	**(Choose ____)**	**(Choose ____)**	**(Choose ____)**
Before Reading ✱On the chart, write three expectations you have of the book.	✱Write a descriptive paragraph about an important person, place, or thing.	✱Find puzzling plurals.	✱Make a setting pyramid showing three important places.
Halfway Point ✱Is the book meeting your expectations? Fill in the chart with reasons.	✱Write three journal entries.	✱Use onomatopoeia in a description.	✱Draw a caricature, or exaggerated portrait, of a character.
After Reading ✱Fill in the rest of the expectations chart. Share your chart with a classmate who has read the same book.	✱Compare yourself to a character.	✱Replace common words with dazzling different ones!	Draw a detailed picture of an important person, place, or thing from your book. Write a few sentences about your drawing.
After Reading ✱Complete a fiction conference form and schedule a conference with your teacher.	✱Write a dialogue.	✱Search for the subject.	Create a new book jacket. Draw a picture on the cover. On the back cover, write a summary of the book and a mini-biography of the author.

Name _____ Date _____

Book Title _____

Expectations Chart

Before reading the book, write three expectations you have for it. Write a reason for each. After you have read half of the book, write if the book is fulfilling each of your expectations. Explain why or why not. After you have finished the book, write if the book fulfilled each expectation and tell why or why not.

Before Reading	Halfway Point	After Reading
Expectation 1 _____ _____ _____ _____ _____	**Expectation 1** _____ _____ _____ _____ _____	**Expectation 1** _____ _____ _____ _____ _____
Expectation 2 _____ _____ _____ _____ _____	**Expectation 2** _____ _____ _____ _____ _____	**Expectation 2** _____ _____ _____ _____ _____
Expectation 3 _____ _____ _____ _____ _____	**Expectation 3** _____ _____ _____ _____ _____	**Expectation 3** _____ _____ _____ _____ _____

Ready-to-Use Independent Reading Management Kit: Grades 4–6 Scholastic Professional Books

Name _____ Date _____

Book Title _____

Descriptive Paragraph

Write a descriptive paragraph about an important person, place, or thing from the story. First, brainstorm a list of details about the person, place, or thing. Then write a carefully constructed paragraph that provides plenty of description.

Details

_____   _____

_____   _____

_____   _____

_____   _____

_____   _____

_____   _____

_____

_____

_____

_____

_____

_____

_____

_____

_____

Name _____ Date _____

Book Title _____

My Journal

Choose three important days in the main character's life. Write a journal entry for each of the days. Remember to write from the character's perspective and to explain why these days were important to the character. Attach additional pages as needed.

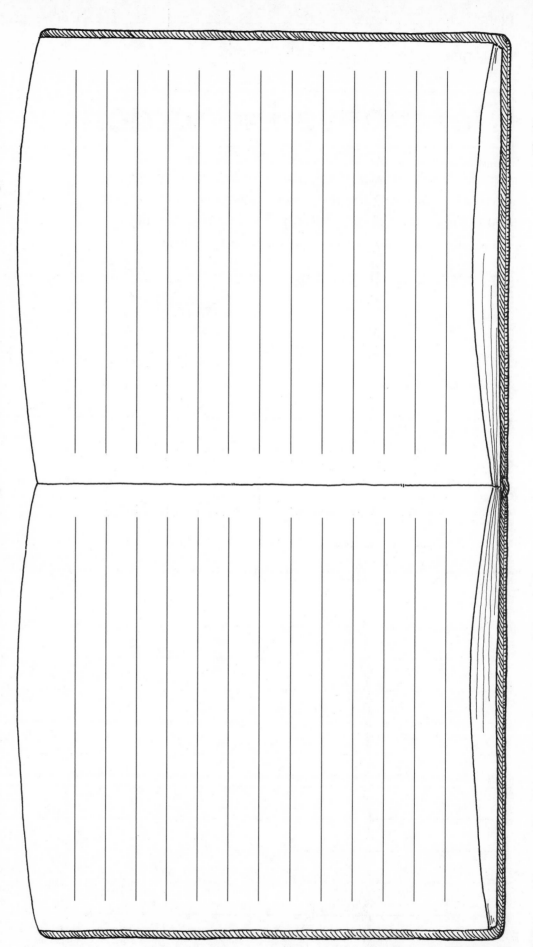

Ready-to-Use Independent Reading Management Kit: Grades 4–6   Scholastic Professional Books

Fiction 3 • Writing

Ready-to-Use Independent Reading Management Kit: Grades 4–6   Scholastic Professional Books

Name _____   Date _____

Book Title _____

Compare Yourself to a Character

Choose a character from your book. Think about how you are alike and different. Fill in the Venn diagram below. Then use the information to write three paragraphs, one for each section of the Venn diagram. Write your paragraphs on a separate sheet of paper and attach it to this sheet.

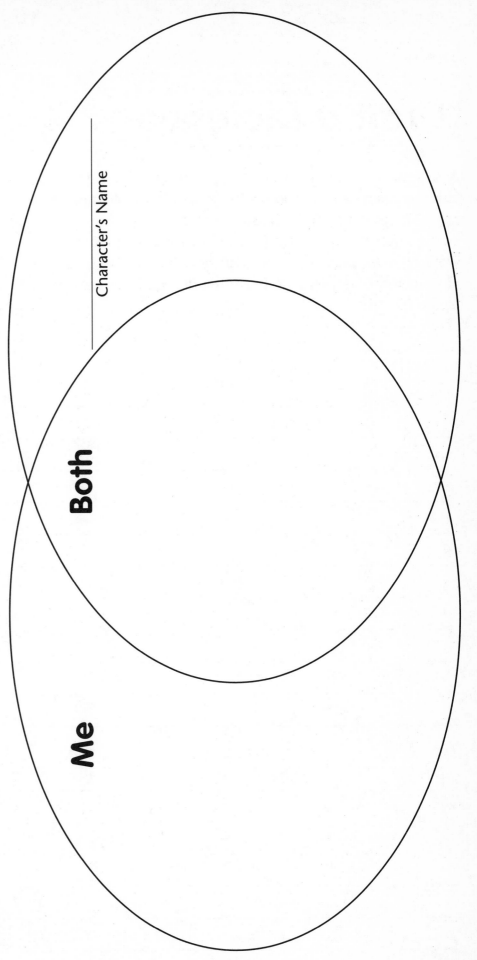

Character's Name

Both

Me

Name_____ Date_____

Book Title_____

Draft a Dialogue

A dialogue is a written conversation between two or more characters. Imagine a dialogue that might have taken place at an interesting point in the story and write it on the lines below. Look at examples in your book before you begin writing. Think about how the characters speak. How is each character's personality revealed in the dialogue? Remember to use quotation marks.

_____

_____

_____

_____

_____

_____

_____

_____

_____

_____

_____

_____

_____

_____

_____

_____

_____

_____

_____

_____

Ready-to-Use Independent Reading Management Kit: Grades 4–6 Scholastic Professional Books

Puzzling Plurals

Most plural nouns are formed by adding the letter *s* to the singular noun. Some plural nouns are more complicated.

Look in your book for nouns whose plural forms require more than just an *s*. (You can look for the noun in either the singular or plural form.) Write the singular form on one puzzle piece and the plural form on the other.

Singular	**Plural**
butterfly	butterflies
elf	elves

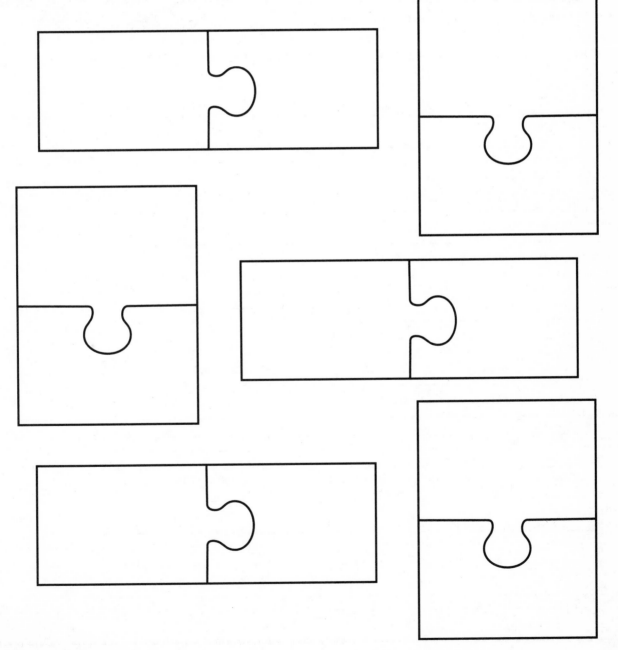

Onomatopoeia

Onomatopoeia is the use of words that sound like what they mean.

EXAMPLES: **whisper   buzz   hiss**

Look for a passage in your book that you could rewrite using onomatopoeia. When you are finished, ask a classmate to read the paragraph aloud and circle the words that sound like their meanings.

_____

_____

_____

_____

_____

_____

_____

_____

_____

_____

_____

_____

_____

_____

Ready-to-Use Independent Reading Management Kit: Grades 4–6   Scholastic Professional Books

Name _____ Date _____

Book Title _____

Dazzling and Different Words

Find a paragraph in your book that uses a lot of common words. Copy the paragraph on the lines below. Then cross out the common words and replace with them dazzling different words! Use a thesaurus to help.

Ready-to-Use Independent Reading Management Kit: Grades 4–6   Scholastic Professional Books

Name _____ Date _____

Book Title _____

Search for the Subject

Copy ten sentences from your book.
Then circle the subject in each one.
Look for at least one sentence that
does not start with the subject.

EXAMPLE: **Last summer, (Leo) went
to camp for the first time.**

1. _____

2. _____

3. _____

4. _____

5. _____

6. _____

7. _____

8. _____

9. _____

10. _____

Ready-to-Use Independent Reading Management Kit: Grades 4–6 Scholastic Professional Books

Fiction 3 • Skills

Setting Pyramid

You will need three copies of the template below. Follow these directions for each sheet:

1. Cut out the square along the solid line.

2. Fold diagonally along the dotted line. Open the paper and fold diagonally the other way.

3. Cut along the solid line.

4. On the uncut half, draw a picture of an important place in the story.

5. On the lines, write where this place is and why it's important.

6. Glue flap 1 on top of flap 2.

7. Glue together the backs of the sections.

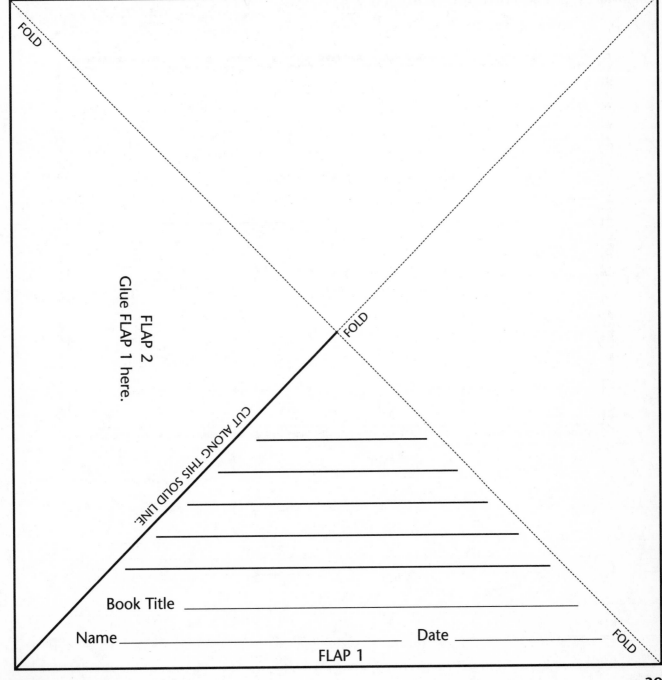

FOLD

FOLD

FOLD

FOLD

FLAP 2
Glue FLAP 1 here.

CUT ALONG THIS SOLID LINE.

Book Title _____

Name _____ Date _____

FLAP 1

Ready-to-Use Independent Reading Management Kit: Grades 4–6   Scholastic Professional Books

Name _____ Date _____

Book Title _____

Character Caricature

A caricature is a cartoon-like drawing that exaggerates features and expressions. It often includes a few objects that tell about the character. Draw a caricature of a character in your book. Underneath the drawing, write the name of the character and describe your caricature. What did you exaggerate and why? Did you include any objects? Why or why not?

_____

_____

_____

_____

_____

_____

Ready-to-Use Independent Reading Management Kit: Grades 4–6   Scholastic Professional Books

Name_____ Date_____

FICTION 4
Independent Reading Contract

Book Title_____

This book was: (easy) **1   2   3   4   5**   (difficult)

Complete the activities based on your independent reading book.
When you have finished an activity, check the box.

Activities marked with an asterisk ✱ have an activity sheet.

Reading	Writing	Skills	Art
(Do all 4.)	**(Choose ____)**	**(Choose ____)**	**(Choose ____)**
Beginning of Book Notice the point of view. Is the story told by an all-knowing narrator or by one of the characters?	✱Write a letter to the author.	✱Create a spelling game with words from your book.	✱Create a coat of arms for a character.
Beginning of Book ✱Look for descriptions that involve the five senses. Write them in your sensory chart.	✱Fill in a plot paragraph.	✱Find linking verbs.	Draw or paint a picture of a main setting in the book. Label those elements that are important to the story.
Halfway Point ✱Continue to fill in your sensory chart. Share your chart with another student.	✱Grade a character. **Friendship A+** **Generosity B–**	✱Unlock the prefixes and root words.	Draw or cut out pictures from magazines that represent the conflict, and glue them onto construction paper to make a collage.
After Reading ✱Complete a fiction conference form and schedule a conference with your teacher.	✱Write character fortune cookies.	✱Fill in a topsy-turvy title sheet. My Side of the Mountain eye tan not noted dome fade tummy distant	Make a poster advertising the theme of the book. Draw several pictures that relate to the theme. Write a caption beneath each.

Ready-to-Use Independent Reading Management Kit: Grades 4–6   Scholastic Professional Books

Name_____ Date _____

Book Title _____

Sensory Chart

Look for descriptions that involve the five senses, such as "the wind whispered through the trees" or "the smell of freshly baked bread filled the house." Write an example from the book for each of the senses. Include the page number for reference.

Sense	Example From Book	Page
Hearing		
Smelling		
Seeing		
Tasting		
Feeling		

Ready-to-Use Independent Reading Management Kit: Grades 4–6   Scholastic Professional Books

Name_____ Date _____

Book Title _____

Letter to the Author

Write a letter to the author of your book. Describe your reactions to the characters, plot, setting, conclusion, and any other part of the story. Include questions for the author about the book and the writing process. You might also include suggestions for a sequel to the book.

Date _____

Dear _____,

_____

_____

_____

_____

_____

_____

_____

_____

_____

_____

_____

_____

Sincerely,

_____

Ready-to-Use Independent Reading Management Kit: Grades 4–6   Scholastic Professional Books

Name_____ Date_____

Book Title _____

Plot Paragraph

The problem in this book begins when _____

_____

_____

After that, _____

_____

Then, _____

_____

Next, _____

_____

Finally, the problem is resolved when _____

_____

_____

At the end of the story, _____

_____

_____

_____

Ready-to-Use Independent Reading Management Kit: Grades 4–6   Scholastic Professional Books

Name _____ Date _____

Book Title _____

Grade a Character

Characters often have strengths and weaknesses. Choose a character from the book. Give the character a grade for each category. Beside the grade, explain why you gave that grade and provide an example to support your explanation.

Character's Name _____

Category	Grade	Explanation and Example
Responsibility		_____ _____
Thoughtfulness		_____ _____
Friendship		_____ _____
Generosity		_____ _____
Sense of humor		_____ _____
Problem solving		_____ _____
Compassion		_____ _____

Name_____ Date _____

Book Title _____

Character Fortune Cookies

Imagine that at the beginning of the book, the main character breaks
open three fortune cookies and reads the fortunes inside. What does the
character learn about his or her future? Write a fortune in each cookie.
On the lines, write what happens in the book to support that fortune.

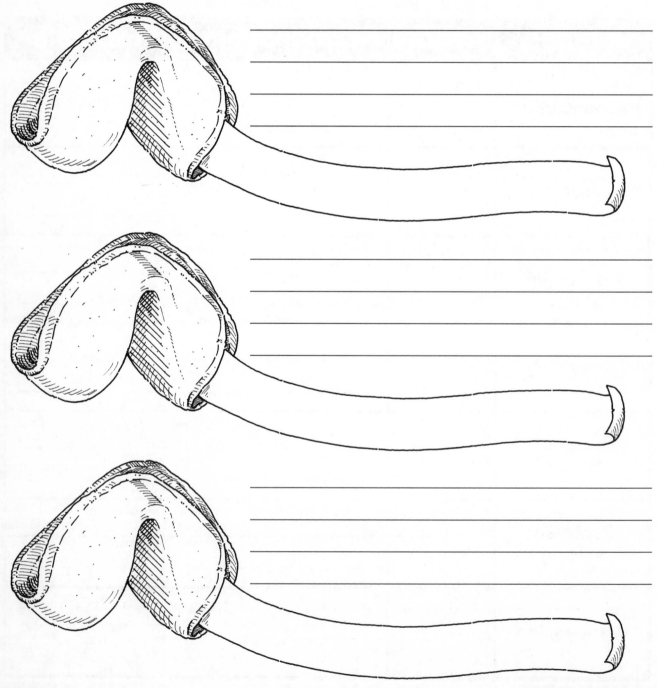

Ready-to-Use Independent Reading Management Kit: Grades 4–6   Scholastic Professional Books

Super Spellers Game

Setup

Look through your book for words that may be difficult to spell. Write a word on each card. Cut out the cards and place them facedown in a pile.

Play (2 players)

One player draws a card and reads the word to the other player. The player who hears the word tries to spell it. If the player spells the word correctly, he or she keeps the card. If not, the card is returned to the bottom of the pile. Players switch roles. When there are no cards left, the player with more cards wins.

Linking Verbs

A linking verb links the subject to its predicate.

EXAMPLES: **I am happy.**   Linking verb = **am** (links *I* to *happy*)

Look in your book for linking verbs. Write the linking verb in
the center link of each chain below. Then write the words that
it links on either side.

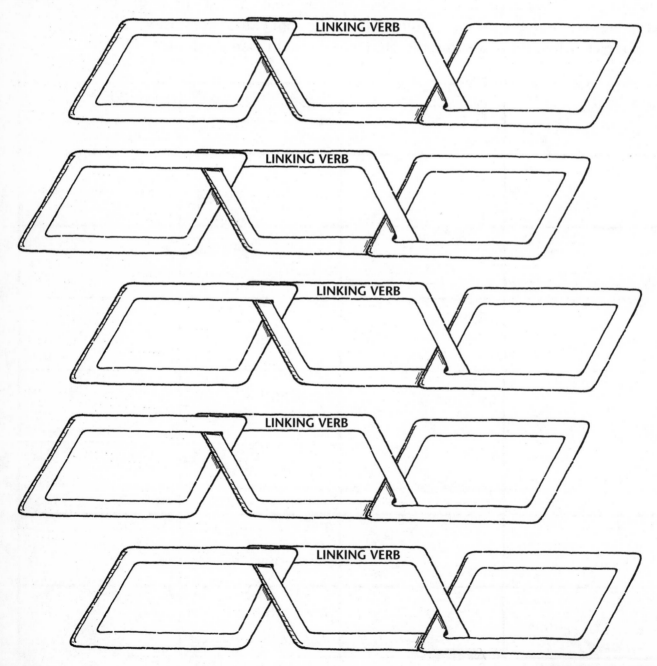

Ready-to-Use Independent Reading Management Kit: Grades 4–6   Scholastic Professional Books

Fiction 4 • Skills

Name _____ Date _____

Book Title _____

Unlock Prefixes and Root Words

Some words have prefixes. The prefix is attached to the beginning of a root word.

EXAMPLE: **unlock**   prefix = **un**   root word = **lock**

Look in your book for words that contain a prefix and root word. Write the prefix on the key and the root word in the lock. Then guess the definition of the word. The first one has been done for you.

Prefix	Root Word	Definition
1. mis	place	to put in the wrong place
2.		
3.		
4.		
5.		
6.		
7.		

Ready-to-Use Independent Reading Management Kit: Grades 4–6   Scholastic Professional Books

Book Title _____

Topsy-Turvy Title

My Side of
the Mountain

eye	tan
not	noted
dome	fade
tummy	distant
this	them

How many words can you create using the letters in your book's
title? (If your title is very short, you can use the letters in the
author's name as well.) First, guess how many words you can make.
Then write the words on the lines and count how many you made.

I think I can make _____ words using the letters in the title.

_____   _____   _____

_____   _____   _____

_____   _____   _____

_____   _____   _____

_____   _____   _____

_____   _____   _____

_____   _____   _____

_____   _____   _____

_____   _____   _____

_____   _____   _____

_____   _____   _____

_____   _____   _____

_____   _____   _____

I made _____ words.

Ready-to-Use Independent Reading Management Kit: Grades 4–6   Scholastic Professional Books

Name_____ Date _____

Book Title _____

Design a coat of arms for a character in your book. In each section of the shield below, draw a picture that shows something about the character.

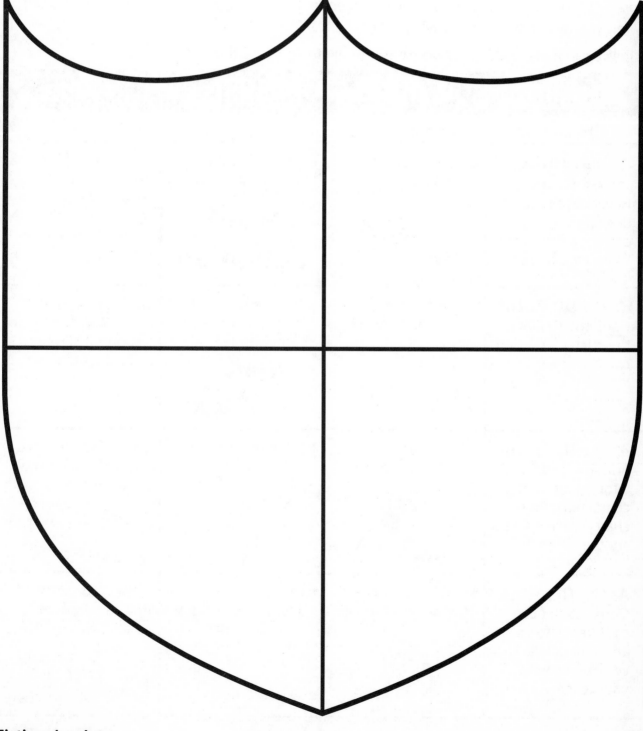

Name_____ Date_____

Independent Reading Contract

Book Title _____

This book was: (easy)   **1**   **2**   **3**   **4**   **5**   (difficult)

Complete the activities based on your independent reading book.
When you have finished an activity, check the box.

Activities marked with an asterisk ✱ have an activity sheet.

Reading	Writing	Skills	Art
(Do all 4.)	**(Choose ____)**	**(Choose ____)**	**(Choose ____)**
Beginning of Book ✱How does the author describe the characters? Fill in the characterization chart.	✱Write an advice column.	✱Make a vocabulary study chart. **word definition**	Create a character quilt. Cut out paper squares. Decorate a square for each character and then tape them together.
Halfway Point ✱Continue to fill in the characterization chart.	✱Create a poster about a character.	✱Write sentences that use pairs of homophones. **here hear**	Draw pictures to create a slide show of important settings from the book.
After Reading ✱Add any additional information to the characterization chart. Share it with another student.	✱Research and write about the author.	✱Think of antonyms for words in your book.	Draw a comic strip that tells about the conflict in the story.
After Reading ✱Complete a fiction conference form and schedule a conference with your teacher.	✱Write about the theme of the book.	✱Think of alternate titles for your book.	Draw a comic strip that tells how the conflict was resolved.

Ready-to-Use Independent Reading Management Kit: Grades 4–6   Scholastic Professional Books

Name _____ Date _____

Book Title _____

Characterization Chart

A writer can reveal aspects of a character's personality in different ways. This is called characterization. Read the examples below, then look for different types of characterization in your book. Write an example of each type.

The writer describes the character.

EXAMPLE: The giant was shy, kind, and generous.

_____

_____

_____

The character says or does something.

EXAMPLE: The giant blushed and said, "I knew you weren't feeling well, so I brought you some of my homemade lizard soup."

_____

_____

_____

Another character thinks or says something about the character.

EXAMPLE: The elf said to the giant, "You may be the most powerful creature in the forest, but you wouldn't hurt a fly."

_____

_____

_____

Ready-to-Use Independent Reading Management Kit: Grades 4–6 Scholastic Professional Books

Name _____ Date _____

Book Title _____

Advice Column

Imagine that you write an advice column for a newspaper. Write a letter from the main character, describing the problem in the story. What would you advise the character to do? Write a letter explaining your solutions. You will need two copies of this sheet.

Name _____ Date _____

Book Title _____

All About a Character

Choose an interesting character from your book. Imagine that you are the character and fill in the poster below. Use the information you know about the character to guess how he or she would fill in the blanks. Draw pictures in the boxes.

Read All About _____!

Character's Name

This is what I look like:

Corner of Favorites

Favorite food: _____

_____

Favorite movie: _____

_____

Favorite song: _____

_____

Favorite hobby: _____

_____

Age: _____

Home: _____

Grade level or occupation: _____

Ambition in life: _____

_____

Someone I admire: _____

Something I would change about myself: _____

_____

An accomplishment I am proud of: _____

_____

Special talent(s): _____

A picture of my favorite person, place, or thing:

Ready-to-Use Independent Reading Management Kit: Grades 4–6   Scholastic Professional Books

Name _____ Date _____

Book Title _____

All About the Author

Look up information about the author of your book and fill in the
blanks below. Then imagine that you are the author. How would
you introduce yourself and what would you tell people about your
life? Prepare a short speech and perform it for the class.

Name: _____

Born: _____ **Still Alive/Died:** _____

Birthplace: _____ **Current hometown:** _____

Important events in author's life: _____

_____

_____

Important people in author's life: _____

_____

_____

Hobbies: _____

_____

Other books by the same author: _____

_____

_____

Author's thoughts about writing or about this particular book: ____

_____

_____

Other interesting information: _____

_____

Ready-to-Use Independent Reading Management Kit: Grades 4–6 Scholastic Professional Books

Name_____ Date _____

Book Title _____

Think About the Theme

My theme is...

The theme is the main idea or message of the whole book. It is different from the subject of the book. For example, the subject of a book could be baseball and the theme could be overcoming obstacles. A book may have more than one theme.

Answer the questions below to help you discover the theme of your book.

What was the most important event in the story?

_____

_____

What did the main character learn from this event?

_____

_____

Did the main character change in any way? How?

_____

_____

_____

**What is important to the main character at the beginning of the book?
At the end of the book?**

_____

_____

_____

Write a sentence or two about the theme of the book:

_____

_____

_____

Ready-to-Use Independent Reading Management Kit: Grades 4–6   Scholastic Professional Books

Name _____ Date _____

Book Title _____

Vocabulary Study Chart

Look in your book for words whose meanings you do not know.
Write the words in the left-hand column. Look up the words in the
dictionary and then write the definitions in the right-hand column.
Cut out the chart. Then fold along the dotted line so that you can
quiz yourself on the definitions without looking at them.

Word	Definition

Ready-to-Use Independent Reading Management Kit: Grades 4–6   Scholastic Professional Books

Homophone Challenge

A homophone is a word that sounds the same as another word but has a different meaning or spelling. Can you think of any homophone pairs? Look through your book for words that are part of a homophone pair. Write each homophone, then write one sentence that uses both homophones.

here
hear

Homophones: _hear_____ _here_____

Sentence: _It's hard to hear in here!_____

Homophones: _____ _____

Sentence: _____

Homophones: _____ _____

Sentence: _____

Homophones: _____ _____

Sentence: _____

Homophones: _____ _____

Sentence: _____

Homophones: _____ _____

Sentence: _____

Homophones: _____ _____

Sentence: _____

Homophones: _____ _____

Sentence: _____

Antonyms All Around

Antonyms are words with opposite meanings. Look for words in your book and then try to think of an antonym for each. Write the word on the left-hand page of the book below and the antonym on the right.

Word

Antonym

Ready-to-Use Independent Reading Management Kit: Grades 4–6   Scholastic Professional Books

Fiction 5 • Skills

Name_____ Date _____

Book Title _____

Title Time

Think of other titles the author might have used for this book. Write a title on each book cover, making sure to capitalize the appropriate words. (A general rule is to capitalize all words except conjunctions, prepositions, and articles. Only capitalize a conjunction, preposition, or article if it is the first or last word in the title or if it's four or more letters long. EXAMPLES: *Gone With the Wind, A House Is a House for Me*)

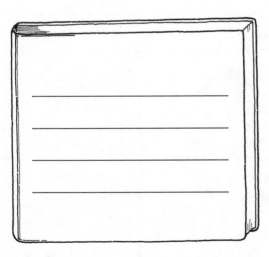

Fiction 5 • Skills

Name_____ Date_____

BIOGRAPHY
Independent Reading Contract

Book Title_____

This book was: (easy) **1   2   3   4   5**   (difficult)

Complete the activities based on your independent reading book.
When you have finished an activity, check the box.

Activities marked with an asterisk ✱ have an activity sheet.

Reading	Writing	Skills	Art
(Do all 4.)	**(Choose _____)**	**(Choose _____)**	**(Choose _____)**
Before Reading ✱Fill in a K-W-L chart (What I **K**now, What I **W**ant to Know, What I **L**earned).	✱Write a letter to the person your biography is about.	✱List adjectives that describe people, places, or things in your book. **noisy clock**	✱Design a postage stamp that honors the subject of the biography.
Halfway Point Find a passage that describes an important accomplishment of the main character. Share it with another student.	✱Construct a time line of the person's life.	✱Find eight irregular verbs in your book.	✱Draw a charm bracelet that the person might have worn. Each charm should represent an accomplishment or interest.
After Reading ✱Complete the K-W-L chart.	✱Make a character web.	✱Make your own mini thesaurus.	Make a museum in a box. Decorate the inside of a shoe box to create a 3-D display of an important event in the person's life.
After Reading ✱Complete a biography conference form and schedule a conference with your teacher.	✱Write a speech about the person in your book.	✱Create a name search for a classmate to solve.	Use modeling clay to create a bust resembling the person you read about. (If clay is not available, draw a portrait.)

Ready-to-Use Independent Reading Management Kit: Grades 4–6 Scholastic Professional Books

Name_____ Date _____

Book Title _____

K-W-L Chart: Biography

Before you begin reading your book, fill in the first two columns of the chart. First, write what you know about the subject of the biography. Then write what you want to know about this person. After you finish the book, write what you learned.

Know	Want to Know	Learned
_____	_____	_____
_____	_____	_____
_____	_____	_____
_____	_____	_____
_____	_____	_____
_____	_____	_____
_____	_____	_____
_____	_____	_____
_____	_____	_____
_____	_____	_____
_____	_____	_____
_____	_____	_____
_____	_____	_____
_____	_____	_____
_____	_____	_____
_____	_____	_____

Ready-to-Use Independent Reading Management Kit: Grades 4–6   Scholastic Professional Books

Biography • Reading

Name_____ Date _____

Book Title _____

Write a Letter

Write a letter to the person your biography is about. If you need additional room, attach another sheet of paper. Here are some ideas for what you might include in your letter.

- What would you like to ask the person?
- What do you admire about the person?
- What do you have in common with the person?
- What current events might interest the person if he or she is no longer alive?
- What advice would you give the person about a problem he or she faced in the book?

_____

Dear _____ ,

_____

_____

_____

_____

_____

_____

_____

Sincerely,

_____

Ready-to-Use Independent Reading Management Kit: Grades 4–6 Scholastic Professional Books

Biography • Writing

Name _____

Date _____

Book Title _____

Time Line

Make a time line about the biography you read. What events happened in the person's life? Write them in the order they occurred, and include some information about each event. Cut along the lines shown and then tape the two strips together.

Some events to consider including:

• date and place of birth

• important accomplishments

• marriage and birth of children

Name _____ Date _____

Book Title _____

Character Web

Write the name of the person in the center of the web. Think of three qualities or characteristics that describe the person (generous, forgiving, and so on). Write the qualities in the ovals. Then think of two examples from the biography that show each quality. Write the examples in the boxes.

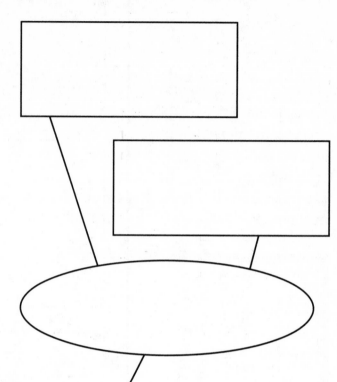

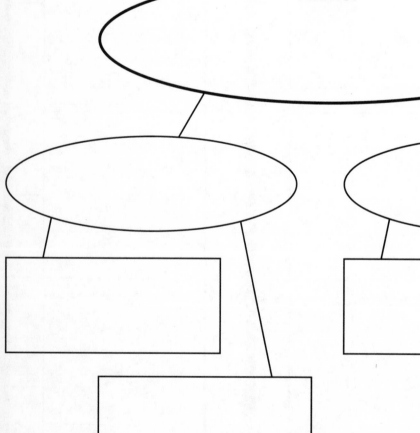

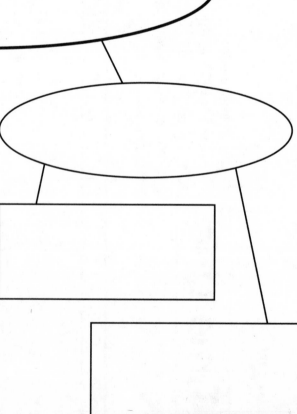

Name:

Ready-to-Use Independent Reading Management Kit: Grades 4–6 Scholastic Professional Books

Biography • Writing

tle _____

ini Thesaurus

en words from your book and write them in
petical order. Then think of as many synonyms
can for each and write them on the lines. Use
aurus or dictionary to find even more synonyms
d to the list. An example has been done for you.

Word   ## Synonyms

intelligent   smart, clever, brilliant, intellectual, knowledgeable

_____   _____

_____   _____

_____   _____

. _____   _____

. _____   _____

7. _____   _____

8. _____   _____

9. _____   _____

10. _____   _____

Ready-to-Use Independent Reading Management Kit: Grades 4–6   Scholastic Professional Books

---

Book Title _____

Write a Speech

Imagine that you are going to deliver a speech
praising the person your biography is about. Include
information about that person's important
accomplishments and praiseworthy qualities. Include
examples from the book that demonstrate these
qualities.

_____

_____

_____

_____

_____

_____

_____

_____

_____

_____

_____

_____

_____

_____

_____

_____

Ready-to-Use Independent Reading Management Kit: Grades 4–6   Scholastic Professional Books

Name _____ Date _____

Book Title _____

Adjectives All Around

An adjective is a word that describes a person, place, or thing.

Find adjectives in your book. In the chart below, write the adjectives and the words they describe. Then think of a different adjective to describe the same word.

People	Places	Things
adjective from book: _courageous astronaut_ new adjective: _cheerful astronaut_	adjective from book: _inviting house_ new adjective: _mysterious house_	adjective from book: _noisy clock_ new adjective: _broken clock_
adjective from book: _____ new adjective: _____	adjective from book: _____ new adjective: _____	adjective from book: _____ new adjective: _____
adjective from book: _____ new adjective: _____	adjective from book: _____ new adjective: _____	adjective from book: _____ new adjective: _____
adjective from book: _____ new adjective: _____	adjective from book: _____ new adjective: _____	adjective from book: _____ new adjective: _____

Biography • Skills

Name _____ Date _____

Book Title _____

Irregular Verbs

An irregular verb does not follow the rule of adding *-ed* to form the past tense.

EXAMPLE:

Regular Verb	**Irregular Verb**
present tense = **jump**	present tense = **fly**
past tense = **jumped**	past tense = **flew**

Look in your biography for ten irregular verbs. They can be in either the present or past tense. Write the verb in the appropriate column and then fill in the other column.

Present Tense   Past Te[nse]

1. _____   _____

2. _____   _____

3. _____   _____

4. _____   _____

5. _____   _____

6. _____   _____

7. _____   _____

8. _____   _____

9. _____   _____

10. _____   _____

Biography • Skills

Name _____

Book Ti[tle]

M

Find te
alphab
as you
a thes
to add

1.

2.

3.

4

5

Name Search

On a piece of scrap paper, make a list of characters' names from your book. Then fit as many names as you can into the grid. You can place the words vertically, horizontally, or diagonally. Write clues for each character below. Then fill in the blank spaces with additional letters. Challenge a classmate who has read the book to find and circle the names.

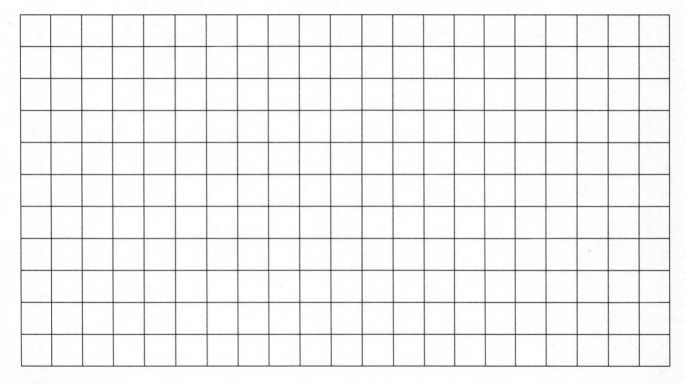

Clues

_____

_____

_____

_____

_____

_____

Postage Stamp

Postage stamps are sometimes designed to honor a person. What would a stamp honoring the person in your book look like? You might include a picture of the person as well as any objects that represent his or her accomplishments. After sketching the stamp on scrap paper, draw your stamp in the space below. Beneath it, explain the design of your stamp.

_____

_____

_____

Ready-to-Use Independent Reading Management Kit: Grades 4–6   Scholastic Professional Books

Biography • Art

Charm Bracelet

Sometimes people collect charms to add to a bracelet. Each charm is a small piece of jewelry that represents something important to the person. A charm could be a tiny tennis racquet, a heart, or even the Eiffel Tower. The charms on a bracelet can reveal a lot about the person it belongs to.

Design a charm bracelet for the person in the book. Include at least ten charms and draw a picture of each. On a separate sheet of paper, write a paragraph explaining what these charms tell about that person's life or interests.

Name_____ Date_____

MYSTERY
Independent Reading Contract

Book Title _____

This book was: (easy) **1** **2** **3** **4** **5** (difficult)

Complete the activities based on your independent reading book.
When you have finished an activity, check the box.

Activities marked with an asterisk ✱ have an activity sheet.

Reading	Writing	Skills	Art
(Do all 4.)	**(Choose ____)**	**(Choose ____)**	**(Choose ____)**
Beginning of Book ✱How do you feel about the characters at the beginning of the book? Fill in the character chart.	✱Compose character limericks.	✱Interrogate with interrogatives. (Ask questions!) **??????**	Draw an invention that a character might have needed. Then write what it does and how the character would have used it.
Halfway Point ✱How do you feel about the characters at the middle of the book? Fill in the character chart.	✱Find real and false clues.	✱Find words that follow and break the spelling rule "*i* before *e* except after *c*."	Draw a floor plan of a building in which important story events occurred. Label the areas and write what events happened in each.
After Reading ✱How do you feel about the characters at the end of the book? Fill in the character chart.	✱What makes a mystery? Answer questions to find out. **?**	✱Discover as many conjunctions as you can. **and so or if**	Create a fingerprint picture of a scene from your mystery. Use an inkpad and your fingers!
After Reading ✱Complete a mystery conference form and schedule a conference with your teacher.	✱Set the mood in a paragraph that describes a setting.	✱Create a secret code about your book.	Imagine that the mystery is being made into a movie. Choose three characters and design a costume for each.

Ready-to-Use Independent Reading Management Kit: Grades 4–6   Scholastic Professional Books

Ready-to-Use Independent Reading Management Kit: Grades 4–6   Scholastic Professional Books

Name _____   Date _____

Book Title _____

Character Chart

What do you think of the characters at the beginning of the story? How do you feel about them at the middle and end of the story? Choose three important characters. Fill in the chart below with your impressions of these characters at the beginning, middle, and end of the book.

Character	Beginning	Middle	End

Character Limericks

A limerick is a humorous poem with the following guidelines:

- It has five lines.
- Lines 1, 2, and 5 rhyme and have three stressed syllables.
- Lines 3 and 4 rhyme and have two stressed syllables.
- Line 1 often starts with the phrase "There once was…"

Read the example aloud several times to get a feeling for the rhythm.

> **There once was a kid in fifth grade,**
> **who lived his life unafraid.**
> **His fear was unknown**
> **until he was thrown**
> **when his homework was boldly displayed.**

Now write your own limericks! Choose two characters
and write a limmerick about each of them.

Character's Name _____

_____

_____

_____

_____

_____

Character's Name _____

_____

_____

_____

_____

_____

Ready-to-Use Independent Reading Management Kit: Grades 4–6 Scholastic Professional Books

Mystery • Writing

Name_____ Date _____

Book Title _____

Find the Clues

Throughout a mystery, the writer provides the reader with clues.
Some of the clues help the reader figure out the ending. Other clues
lead the reader in the wrong direction in order to conceal the ending.
Look through your mystery for examples of real clues and false clues.

_____   _____

_____   _____

_____   _____

_____   _____

_____   _____

_____   _____

_____   _____

_____   _____

_____   _____

_____   _____

_____   _____

_____   _____

_____   _____

Ready-to-Use Independent Reading Management Kit: Grades 4–6   Scholastic Professional Books

Book Title _____

What Makes a Mystery?

What makes a mystery different from other fictional books?
Think about the story elements below. Then answer the
questions, providing examples to support your ideas.

Characters:

Are any of the characters mysterious? In what ways? _____

_____

_____

_____

Plot:

What is the problem that needs to be solved?_____

_____

_____

Is the plot suspenseful? In what ways? _____

_____

_____

Conclusion:

How is the problem solved? _____

_____

_____

Were there any surprises at the end of the book? _____

_____

_____

Ready-to-Use Independent Reading Management Kit: Grades 4–6 Scholastic Professional Books

Mystery • Writing

Name _____ Date _____

Book Title _____

Set the Mood

Think about how the setting determines the mood or atmosphere of a story. Look through your book for a passage that describes the setting. How does the description make you feel?

Now make up your own setting and decide how you want your reader to feel. Anxious? Excited? Content? Think about how you can describe it to make your reader feel a certain way. Remember not to tell your reader how to feel. Instead, make the reader feel a certain way by writing an effective description.

_____

_____

_____

_____

_____

_____

_____

_____

_____

_____

_____

_____

_____

_____

_____

_____

Interrogate With Interrogatives!

Interrogative is a fancy word for a question. When you interrogate someone, you ask the person a lot of questions.

Look in your book for five statements and write them on the lines. Then change each statement into a question.

EXAMPLE: Statement: **The detective was the first to arrive at the crime scene.**

Interrogative: **Was the detective the first to arrive at the crime scene?**

1. Statement: _____

Interrogative: _____

2. Statement: _____

Interrogative: _____

3. Statement: _____

Interrogative: _____

4. Statement: _____

Interrogative: _____

5. Statement: _____

Interrogative: _____

Ready-to-Use Independent Reading Management Kit: Grades 4–6   Scholastic Professional Books

Mystery • Skills

Follow the Rules!

Find eight words in your book that follow this spelling
rule and write them on the lines.

**Put *i* before *e* except after *c* and when sounded
like *a* as in *neighbor* and *weigh*.**

Follows the Rule

_____

_____

_____

_____

_____

_____

_____

Can you find one word that breaks
the rule? Write it in the box. (If you
cannot find a word in your book,
think of a word on your own.)

Breaks the Rule

Ready-to-Use Independent Reading Management Kit: Grades 4–6 Scholastic Professional Books

Name _____ Date _____

Book Title _____

Discovering Conjunctions

A conjunction connects words or groups of words.

EXAMPLES:

and	so
or	if
but	than
for	because
nor	unless
yet	although

How many conjunctions can you find in a page or two of your book? Write them in the magnifying glass. Then write your own sentence, using as many conjunctions as you can. (It can be a long sentence!)

Sentence:

_____

_____

Ready-to-Use Independent Reading Management Kit: Grades 4–6 Scholastic Professional Books

Mystery • Skills

Name _____ Date _____

Book Title _____

Secret Code

Create a secret code at the bottom of the page. Think of a number, letter, or symbol to represent each letter. For example:

A = 1	A = B	A = ●
B = 3	B = C	B = ■
C = 5	C = D	C = ❤

Then write a short message about your book in the secret code. Fold the paper along the dotted line to hide the key and challenge a classmate to crack the code!

Write your message here:

Write your code key below this line. Fold the paper up along the dotted line to hide the key.

A = _____   G = _____   N = _____   U = _____

B = _____   H = _____   O = _____   V = _____

C = _____   I = _____   P = _____   W = _____

D = _____   J = _____   Q = _____   X = _____

E = _____   K = _____   R = _____   Y = _____

F = _____   L = _____   S = _____   Z = _____

M = _____   T = _____

Name_____ Date_____

Independent Reading Contract

Book Title _____

This book was: (easy) **1 2 3 4 5** (difficult)

Complete the activities based on your independent reading book.
When you have finished an activity, check the box.

Activities marked with an asterisk ✱ have an activity sheet.

Reading	Writing	Skills	Art
(Do all 4.)	**(Choose ____)**	**(Choose ____)**	**(Choose ____)**
Beginning of Book ✱Look for metaphors and similes in your book. Write them on the chart.	✱Predict the future.	✱Think of synonyms for the word *said*.	Draw a picture that represents the conflict of the book. Then draw a picture that shows how the conflict was resolved.
Halfway Point ✱Continue to fill in the metaphor and simile chart.	✱Describe how the main character changes.	✱Fill in a noun-to-pronoun chart.	Imagine that you're the set designer for a movie about your book. Draw three different sets that reflect important places in the book.
After Reading Share your chart with another student.	✱Find meaningful quotations. **66 99**	✱Retell part of the book as a rhyme! **Word Family** -AY / day / may / play / say	Design a magazine cover about the theme. Draw a picture. Then write the magazine name and article titles that relate to the theme.
After Reading ✱Complete a realistic fiction conference form and schedule a conference with your teacher.	✱What obstacles does the main character face? How does he or she overcome them?	✱Vary your sentence structure.	Use clay to create an important object from the story. (If clay is unavailable, draw a picture instead.)

Ready-to-Use Independent Reading Management Kit: Grades 4–6   Scholastic Professional Books

Name_____ Date _____

Book Title _____

Metaphor and Simile Chart

A simile compares two things, using *like* or *as*.

 EXAMPLE: **The alarm clock blared like a siren.**

A metaphor is a word or phrase that directly compares two things. It does not use *like* or *as*.

 EXAMPLE: **The cat's eyes were glowing embers in the dark.**

Find metaphors and similes in your book. Write them below, along with the page numbers on which you found them.

Metaphors	Similes
page _____ _____	page _____ _____
_____	_____
_____	_____
page _____ _____	page _____ _____
_____	_____
_____	_____
page _____ _____	page _____ _____
_____	_____
_____	_____
page _____ _____	page _____ _____
_____	_____
_____	_____

Predict the Future

Imagine that you are a fortune-teller and the main character pays you a visit. The character wants to know what will happen to him or her after the end of the book. What questions might the character ask about the future? Write the questions and then write your predictions for the future.

Character's name: _____

Character's question: _____

_____

Your prediction: _____

_____

_____

Character's question: _____

_____

Your prediction: _____

_____

_____

Character's question: _____

_____

Your prediction: _____

_____

_____

Character's question: _____

_____

Your prediction: _____

_____

Ready-to-Use Independent Reading Management Kit: Grades 4–6   Scholastic Professional Books

Realistic Fiction • Writing

Name_____ Date _____

Book Title _____

Character Changes

The main character of a book often changes in some way—for example, the character might learn something new, become better at something, or learn to appreciate something. How does the main character in your story change? Draw a picture of the character looking in the mirror at the beginning of the story. Write a description of the character next to the mirror.

Then draw a picture in the second mirror, showing how the character changed. (You might show this through the character's expression or body position, or by adding objects or other people to the picture.) Then describe the change in writing. Include information about what caused this change.

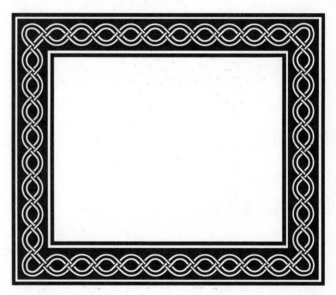

Realistic Fiction • Writing

Quotable Quotations

Look in your book for quotations that give the reader important information about the characters, plot, or theme. Write a quotation in each speech balloon. Then write the name of the character who made the statement. Finally, write why you think this is an important quotation. What information does it provide?

_____
_____
_____

Name of character:

_____

This is important because _____

_____

_____
_____
_____

Name of character:

_____

This is important because _____

_____

_____
_____
_____

Name of character:

_____

This is important because _____

_____

Ready-to-Use Independent Reading Management Kit: Grades 4–6 Scholastic Professional Books

Name _____ Date _____

Book Title _____

Overcoming Obstacles

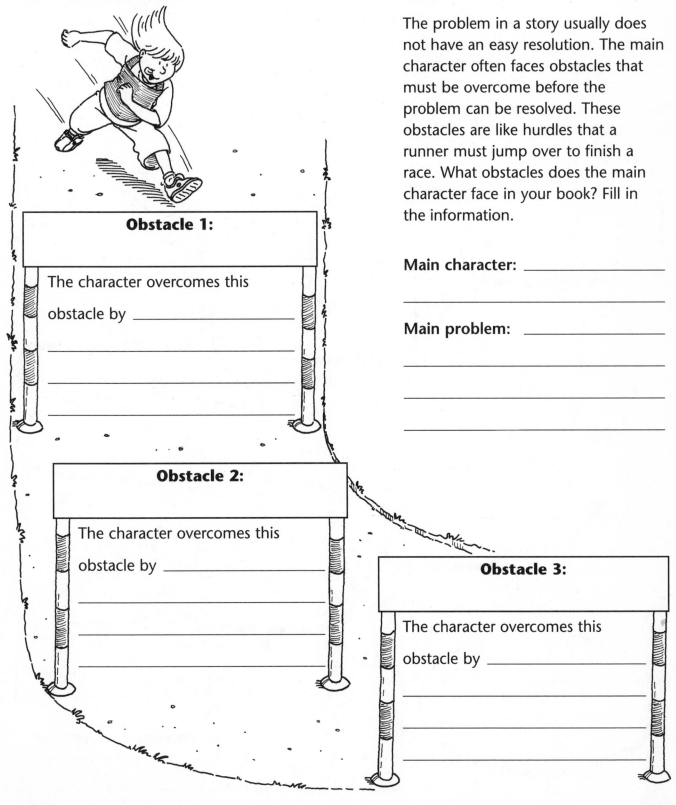

The problem in a story usually does not have an easy resolution. The main character often faces obstacles that must be overcome before the problem can be resolved. These obstacles are like hurdles that a runner must jump over to finish a race. What obstacles does the main character face in your book? Fill in the information.

Main character: _____

_____

Main problem: _____

_____

_____

_____

Obstacle 1:

The character overcomes this

obstacle by _____

_____

_____

_____

Obstacle 2:

The character overcomes this

obstacle by _____

_____

_____

Obstacle 3:

The character overcomes this

obstacle by _____

_____

_____

_____

Ready-to-Use Independent Reading Management Kit: Grades 4–6 Scholastic Professional Books

Name_____ Date _____

Book Title _____

Synonyms for Said

To make dialogue more interesting, writers use other verbs instead of *said*. Look in your book for synonyms for *said* and write them in the speech balloons. Add any other synonyms you can think of, and look in a thesaurus for even more.

shouted

whispered

Ready-to-Use Independent Reading Management Kit: Grades 4–6   Scholastic Professional Books

Name_____ Date _____

Book Title _____

Noun-to-Pronoun Chart

A pronoun is a word that replaces a noun. Copy any sentence from your book. From that sentence, choose one noun that you could change to a pronoun. Write the noun and pronoun in the appropriate columns. Fill in the chart with nine different sentences. Try to use as many different pronouns as you can.

Sentence	Noun	Pronoun
Joey handed the plate to Sheila.	plate	it

Ready-to-Use Independent Reading Management Kit: Grades 4–6 Scholastic Professional Books

Retell in Rhyme!

Choose a part of the story to retell as a rhyme. First, choose a few word families (words that share the same ending) and brainstorm lists of words that belong to each. Then use the words from one or more of the word families to help you write your rhyme. The first one has been started for you.

Word Family	Word Family	Word Family	Word Family
-AY			
day			
may			
play			
say			

Write your rhyme here.

_____

_____

_____

_____

_____

_____

_____

_____

Realistic Fiction • Skills

Ready-to-Use Independent Reading Management Kit: Grades 4–6   Scholastic Professional Books

Book Title _____

Sentence Structure

Writers vary the structure of their sentences to make their
writing more interesting. Look through your book and
notice how the author does this. Writers often vary the
way a sentence begins, making sure some sentences do
not start with the subject. Look for sentences that start
with the subject and try to rewrite them so that they start
in a different way. You may add words if you like.

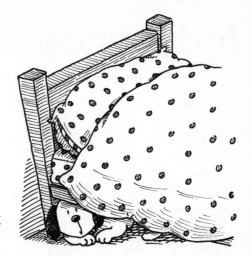

EXAMPLE: sentence from book: **Simon hid under the bed for hours.**
new sentence: **For hours, Simon hid under the bed.**

Sentence from book: _____

  New sentence: _____

Sentence from book: _____

  New sentence: _____

Sentence from book: _____

  New sentence: _____

Sentence from book: _____

  New sentence: _____

Sentence from book: _____

  New sentence: _____

Sentence from book: _____

  New sentence: _____

Realistic Fiction • Skills • 93

Name_____ Date_____

Independent Reading Contract

Book Title _____

This book was: (easy) **1   2   3   4   5** (difficult)

Complete the activities based on your independent reading book.
When you have finished an activity, check the box.

Activities marked with an asterisk ✱ have an activity sheet.

Reading	Writing	Skills	Art
(Do all 4.)	**(Choose ____)**	**(Choose ____)**	**(Choose ____)**
Beginning of Book ✱Write about the introduction on the plot-peak sheet.	✱Write your own chapter.	✱Create a word-search challenge using proper nouns from the book.	Make a travel brochure showing the settings in your book. Write captions for the pictures to entice readers to visit these places.
After Reading ✱Write about the climax on the plot-peak sheet.	✱Explain the main character's goals.	✱Complete a clever clovers sheet with interesting words.	Design toys or action figures based on characters or objects from your story. Write catchy descriptions of each.
After Reading ✱Write about the resolution on the plot-peak sheet.	✱Write a song about your book.	✱Write a dramatic dialogue using interjections.	Make a mobile about your book. Draw or cut out pictures and use string to hang them from a coat hanger.
After Reading ✱Complete an adventure conference form and schedule a conference with your teacher.	✱Describe the most exciting part.	✱Build a vocabulary wall with new verbs from your book.	Create a short children's book that illustrates the main events of the story. You might make it a wordless picture book.

Ready-to-Use Independent Reading Management Kit: Grades 4–6   Scholastic Professional Books

• Adventure

Ready-to-Use Independent Reading Management Kit: Grades 4–6 Scholastic Professional Books

Name _____

Date _____

Book Title _____

Plot Peak

The three main parts of a story are the introduction, climax, and resolution. What happens in each part? Answer the questions.

Introduction

Who are the main characters?

_____

_____

What is the main conflict?

_____

_____

Climax

How is the conflict resolved?

_____

Resolution

What happens after the problem is resolved?

_____

Name_____ Date _____

Book Title _____

Write Your Own Chapter

Think of an event that would make your book even more interesting. Then write a chapter describing the event. Try to write in a style similar to that of the author. In the box, draw a picture to go with your chapter. Add extra pages as needed.

Chapter Title

_____

_____

_____

_____

_____

_____

_____

_____

_____

_____

_____

_____

_____

_____

_____

_____

Ready-to-Use Independent Reading Management Kit: Grades 4–6 Scholastic Professional Books

Goal Checklist

What do you think are the goals of the main character? What
does the main character want to accomplish or learn? Think of
one or two goals and write them below. Then write beside each
one how the character tried to reach the goal and whether he or
she was successful. Write from the point of view of the character.

My Goal	How I Tried to Reach My Goal	Was I Successful?

Name_____ Date _____

Book Title _____

Song Lyrics

Write the lyrics, or words, of a song about your adventure book.
You can set the song to a familiar tune (for example, it could be a
theme song from a television show). In the lyrics, include
information about the characters, setting, and plot. You might even
include a chorus, or a section of the song that repeats. Teach the
song to a classmate and perform it for the class!

_____

_____

_____

_____

_____

_____

_____

_____

_____

_____

_____

_____

Ready-to-Use Independent Reading Management Kit: Grades 4–6   Scholastic Professional Books

Adventure • Writing

Name _____ Date _____

Book Title _____

Most Exciting Part

What was the most exciting part of the book?
Reread the passage and then fill in the information.

Who is involved?

_____

_____

_____

_____

_____

_____

_____

Where and when does it take place?

_____

_____

_____

What happens?

_____

_____

_____

_____

_____

_____

_____

_____

_____

_____

How do the characters feel?

_____

_____

_____

_____

_____

_____

_____

_____

_____

Choose an exciting sentence and write it here:

_____

_____

Ready-to-Use Independent Reading Management Kit: Grades 4–6 Scholastic Professional Books

Name _____ Date _____

Book Title _____

Word-Search Challenge

A proper noun names a particular person, place, or thing and is capitalized. Make a list of proper nouns from your book. Then fit as many as you can into the grid. You can place the words vertically, horizontally, or diagonally. Write the words in the word bank. Then fill in the blank spaces with additional letters. Challenge a classmate to find and circle the words.

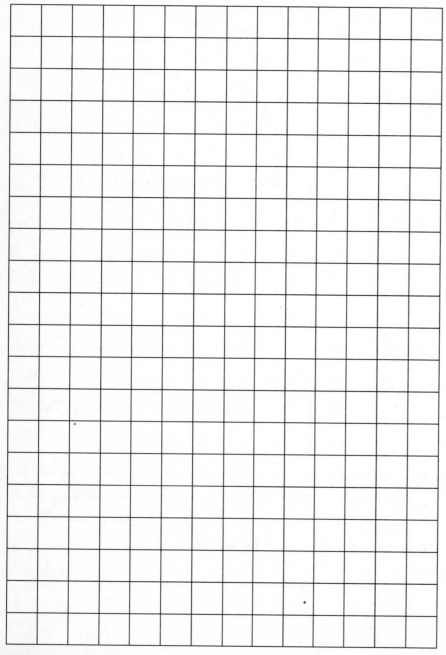

Word Bank

Ready-to-Use Independent Reading Management Kit: Grades 4–6   Scholastic Professional Books

Adventure • Skills

Clever Clovers

Retire boring, overused words! Look in your
book for words that are not very interesting.
Write each of these words on the stem of
one clover. Then think of four interesting
synonyms that could be used instead. Write
each synonym on a petal. Next time you
need an interesting word, pick one of these!

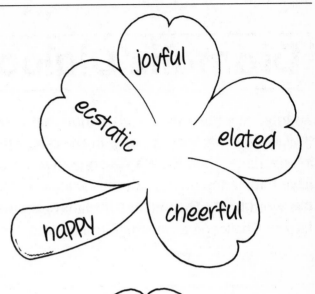

Dramatic Dialogue

An interjection is a brief exclamation that expresses emotion
("*Wow!*" "*Terrific!*" "*Oh, no!*"). In the box, write a list of
interjections. Then write a dialogue that the characters might
have had at any point in the story. Include interjections to make
the dialogue more dramatic. Be sure to use quotation marks.

Ready-to-Use Independent Reading Management Kit: Grades 4–6 Scholastic Professional Books

Name _____

Date _____

Book Title _____

Vocabulary Wall

Look through your book for verbs whose meanings you don't know. In each brick, write a verb and its definition. Then use the verb in a sentence.

Verb: _____

Definition: _____

Sentence: _____

Verb: _____

Definition: _____

Sentence: _____

Verb: _____

Definition: _____

Sentence: _____

Verb: _____

Definition: _____

Sentence: _____

Verb: _____

Definition: _____

Sentence: _____

Verb: _____

Definition: _____

Sentence: _____

Name_____ Date_____

Independent Reading Contract

Book Title _____

This book was: (easy) **1   2   3   4   5**   (difficult)

Complete the activities based on your independent reading book.
When you have finished an activity, check the box.

Activities marked with an asterisk ✱ have an activity sheet.

Reading	Writing	Skills	Art
(Do all 4.)	**(Choose ____)**	**(Choose ____)**	**(Choose ____)**
Before Reading ✱Fill in a K-W-L chart (What I **K**now, What I **W**ant to Know, What I **L**earned).	✱Write a one-paragraph report on a topic from your book.	✱Look for three resources about a topic in your book. Write a brief description of each resource.	Make a 3-D display about the topic of your book. Find objects (or draw pictures) that represent or relate to the topic.
Halfway Point Share with a classmate three interesting facts you've learned.	✱Write about an important lesson learned.	✱Look in your book for strong topic sentences.	Draw a map and label the important places in the book. Draw a small picture that represents what happened in each place.
After Reading ✱Complete the K-W-L chart.	✱Look for cause and effect. Cause → Effect	✱Look in your book for strong concluding sentences.	Draw five pictures that show important events in the book. Cut them out and write on the back what each picture shows.
After Reading ✱Complete a nonfiction conference form and schedule a conference with your teacher.	✱Make fact-or-fiction puzzle pieces. Fact | Fiction	✱Try to reach the moon in a game about verbs and adverbs.	Create a mural on a sheet of craft paper. Write facts that you learned and draw a picture of each.

Ready-to-Use Independent Reading Management Kit: Grades 4–6   Scholastic Professional Books

Name _____ Date _____

Book Title _____

K-W-L Chart: Nonfiction

Before you begin reading your book, fill in the first two columns of the chart. First, write facts that you know about the subject of the book. Then write what you want to know about this subject. After you finish the book, write what you learned.

Know	Want to Know	Learned

Ready-to-Use Independent Reading Management Kit: Grades 4–6 Scholastic Professional Books

Name_____ Date _____

Book Title _____

Paragraph Report

Choose a topic from your book, such as a person, place, invention, or event. Look up information on your topic and write a paragraph about it. Remember that a paragraph should have a topic sentence, at least three supporting facts, and a concluding sentence.

Topic Sentence:

_____

_____

_____

Fact 1:

_____

_____

_____

Fact 2:

_____

_____

_____

Fact 3:

_____

_____

_____

Concluding Sentence

_____

_____

_____

Ready-to-Use Independent Reading Management Kit: Grades 4–6   Scholastic Professional Books

Nonfiction • Writing

Name _____ Date _____

Book Title _____

Lesson Learned

Think about an important lesson that a character learned in your book. How did the character learn the lesson? Why was this important? Did learning the lesson affect the way the character acted afterward? Write a paragraph about the lesson and include a topic sentence, examples to support the topic sentence, and a concluding sentence.

Ready-to-Use Independent Reading Management Kit: Grades 4–6 Scholastic Professional Books

Book Title _____

Cause and Effect

An event that makes something else happen is called a cause.
What happens as a result of an event is called an effect. Find
four examples of cause and effect. Describe the events in the
appropriate boxes.

Cause → **Effect**
_____   _____
_____   _____
_____   _____

Cause → **Effect**
_____   _____
_____   _____
_____   _____

Cause → **Effect**
_____   _____
_____   _____
_____   _____

Cause → **Effect**
_____   _____
_____   _____
_____   _____

Ready-to-Use Independent Reading Management Kit: Grades 4–6   Scholastic Professional Books

Nonfiction • Writing

Book Title _____

Fact-or-Fiction Puzzle

Think of facts that you learned from your book. On one puzzle piece, write a fact. On the adjoining puzzle piece, write a fictional statement about the same topic as the fact. Complete the other puzzle pieces in the same way. Then cut apart the pieces. Challenge a classmate who has read the book to match the puzzle pieces.

Fact	**Fiction**	**Fact**	**Fiction**
Fact	**Fiction**	**Fact**	**Fiction**
Fact	**Fiction**	**Fact**	**Fiction**

Nonfiction • Writing

Name_____ Date _____

Book Title _____

Resource Review

Look in your classroom or school library for three resources
(a book, a magazine or newspaper article, and a Web site)
about an important topic in your book. Write a brief description
of each resource. Then rate how informative each resource is.

Book

Title: _____

Author: _____

Publishing Company: _____ Copyright Date:_____

Description: _____

Rating: (Very informative)   5   4   3   2   1   (Not very informative)

Newspaper or Magazine Article

Title of Article:_____

Author: _____

Title of Newspaper or Magazine:_____

Volume Number (if any): _____   Page(s): _____   Date of Publication: _____

Description:_____

Rating: (Very informative)   5   4   3   2   1   (Not very informative)

Web Site

Name of Web Site: _____

Address: _____

Description: _____

Rating: (Very informative)   5   4   3   2   1   (Not very informative)

Ready-to-Use Independent Reading Management Kit: Grades 4–6   Scholastic Professional Books

Nonfiction • Skills

Top Topic Sentences

Look in your book for four strong topic sentences. A topic sentence should introduce the topic of the paragraph and grab the reader's attention. Copy the sentence, then write the topic of the paragraph and why the sentence grabs your attention.

Topic Sentence:

_____

_____

_____

Topic:

_____

Grabs my attention because:

_____

_____

_____

Topic Sentence:

_____

_____

_____

Topic:

_____

Grabs my attention because:

_____

_____

_____

Topic Sentence:

_____

_____

_____

Topic:

_____

Grabs my attention because:

_____

_____

_____

Topic Sentence:

_____

_____

_____

Topic:

_____

Grabs my attention because:

_____

_____

_____

Ready-to-Use Independent Reading Management Kit: Grades 4–6   Scholastic Professional Books

Clever Concluding Sentences

Look in your book for four strong concluding sentences. A concluding sentence should wrap up the paragraph and give the reader a memorable closing idea. Copy the sentence, then write what the paragraph was about and why the concluding sentence worked well.

Concluding Sentence:

_____

_____

_____

Topic:

_____

Worked well because:

_____

_____

Concluding Sentence:

_____

_____

_____

Topic:

_____

Worked well because:

_____

_____

Concluding Sentence:

_____

_____

_____

Topic:

_____

Worked well because:

_____

_____

Concluding Sentence:

_____

_____

_____

Topic:

_____

Worked well because:

_____

_____

Ready-to-Use Independent Reading Management Kit: Grades 4–6 Scholastic Professional Books

Nonfiction • Skills

Reach the Moon Game

Setup

Look in your book for verbs and adverbs. Write either a verb or an adverb in each star. You will need a die and two markers (such as chips or paper squares).

Play

The first player rolls the die and moves ahead that number of stars. If the player lands on a verb, he or she moves ahead one star. If the player lands on an adverb, he or she uses the word in a sentence and stays in the same space. If the player does not use the word correctly, he or she moves back one star. The first player to reach the moon wins!

Ready-to-Use Independent Reading Management Kit: Grades 4–6   Scholastic Professional Books

Conference Form: Fiction

Name _____ Date of Conference _____

Book Title _____

Fiction 1   **Fiction 2**   **Fiction 3**   **Fiction 4**   **Fiction 5**   (Circle one.)

Write responses to the following questions. Be prepared to discuss
your answers at your teacher conference. Bring your book, your
completed activities, and this form to the conference.

Who do you think is the most interesting character? Why?

_____

_____

_____

What is the most difficult part of the book?
What questions do you have about it?

_____

_____

_____

Choose a favorite passage to share at the conference.
Write the page number and explain why you liked this passage.

_____

_____

_____

What is the theme or the main message of the book?

_____

_____

_____

Teacher's Notes:

_____

_____

Ready-to-Use Independent Reading Management Kit: Grades 4–6   Scholastic Professional Books

• **Fiction**

Conference Form: Biography

Name _____ Date of Conference _____

Book Title _____

Write responses to the following questions. Be prepared to discuss
your answers at your teacher conference. Bring your book, your
completed activities, and this form to the conference.

Who is the subject of your biography?
What made you interested in learning more about this person?

_____

_____

_____

What is the person's most important accomplishment? Why?

_____

_____

_____

What is the most difficult part of the book?
What questions do you have about it?

_____

_____

_____

Choose an interesting passage to share at the conference.
Write the page number and explain why you liked this passage.

_____

_____

_____

Teacher's Notes:

_____

_____

Ready-to-Use Independent Reading Management Kit: Grades 4–6   Scholastic Professional Books

Conference Form: Mystery

Name_____ Date of Conference _____

Book Title _____

Write responses to the following questions. Be prepared to discuss your answers at your teacher conference. Bring your book, your completed activities, and this form to the conference.

Were any parts of the book difficult to understand? What questions do you have about them?

_____

_____

_____

Choose a suspenseful part of your mystery to share at the conference. Write the page number and explain why this passage was suspenseful.

_____

_____

_____

Was the setting important to the mystery? Why or why not?

_____

_____

_____

Did the ending surprise you? Why or why not?

_____

_____

_____

Teacher's Notes:

_____

_____

Ready-to-Use Independent Reading Management Kit: Grades 4–6 Scholastic Professional Books

Conference Form: Realistic Fiction

Name_____ Date of Conference _____

Book Title _____

Write responses to the following questions. Be prepared to discuss your answers at your teacher conference. Bring your book, your completed activities, and this form to the conference.

Do you think your book was realistic? Why or why not? Think about character, setting, and plot.

_____

_____

_____

What was the conflict, or problem, in your book?

_____

_____

_____

How was the conflict resolved?

_____

_____

_____

Choose a good description from your book to share at the conference. Write the page number and explain why you liked this description.

_____

_____

_____

_____

Teacher's Notes:

_____

_____

Ready-to-Use Independent Reading Management Kit: Grades 4–6   Scholastic Professional Books

Conference Form: Adventure

Name _____ Date of Conference _____

Book Title _____

Write responses to the following questions. Be prepared to discuss
your answers at your teacher conference. Bring your book, your
completed activities, and this form to the conference.

What was the climax, or most exciting part, of the story?

_____

_____

_____

Choose an action-packed passage to share at the conference.
Write the page number and explain what you liked about this passage.

_____

_____

_____

Think of a character you admire in some way.
What traits do you admire in this character?

_____

_____

_____

Were there any parts of the book that were difficult to understand?
What questions do you have about them?

_____

_____

_____

Teacher's Notes:

_____

_____

Ready-to-Use Independent Reading Management Kit: Grades 4–6   Scholastic Professional Books

Conference Form: Nonfiction

Name _____ Date of Conference _____

Book Title _____

Write responses to the following questions. Be prepared to discuss
your answers at your teacher conference. Bring your book, your
completed activities, and this form to the conference.

What is the subject of your book?
What made you interested in learning about this subject?

_____

_____

_____

What is the most difficult part of the book?
What questions do you have about it?

_____

_____

_____

Choose an interesting passage to share at the conference.
Write the page number and explain why you liked this passage.

_____

_____

_____

Is there anything else you would like to learn about this subject?

_____

_____

_____

Teacher's Notes:
_____
_____

Ready-to-Use Independent Reading Management Kit: Grades 4–6   Scholastic Professional Books

Books I've Read

Date Finished	Title	Author	Genre
1.			
2.			
3.			
4.			
5.			
6.			
7.			
8.			
9.			
10.			
11.			
12.			
13.			

Name _____ Date _____

Independent Reading Contract _____

Book Title _____

Checkout Form

I'm ready to check out my
independent reading contract.

☐ I completed the right number of activities.

☐ I checked over my work.

☐ I stapled my pages in order.

☐ I filled in a self-assessment rubric.

☐ I scheduled a conference with my teacher.

Name _____ Date _____

Independent Reading Contract _____

Book Title _____

Checkout Form

I'm ready to check out my
independent reading contract.

☐ I completed the right number of activities.

☐ I checked over my work.

☐ I stapled my pages in order.

☐ I filled in a self-assessment rubric.

☐ I scheduled a conference with my teacher.

Ready-to-Use Independent Reading Management Kit: Grades 4–6   Scholastic Professional Books

Name_____ Date _____

Independent Reading Contract _____

Book Title_____

Self-Assessment Rubric

	1 Point	2 Points	3 Points	Score
PRESENTATION	Some of my work is neat and organized.	Most of my work is neat and organized.	All of my work is neat and organized.	
QUALITY OF WORK	Some of my work shows thoughtfulness and understanding.	Most of my work shows thoughtfulness and understanding.	All of my work shows thoughtfulness and understanding.	
EFFICIENCY	I took longer than expected to complete my contract.	I completed my contract on time.	I completed my contract sooner than was expected.	

Total Score _____

Name_____ Date _____

Independent Reading Contract _____

Book Title_____

Self-Assessment Rubric

	1 Point	2 Points	3 Points	Score
PRESENTATION	Some of my work is neat and organized.	Most of my work is neat and organized.	All of my work is neat and organized.	
QUALITY OF WORK	Some of my work shows thoughtfulness and understanding.	Most of my work shows thoughtfulness and understanding.	All of my work shows thoughtfulness and understanding.	
EFFICIENCY	I took longer than expected to complete my contract.	I completed my contract on time.	I completed my contract sooner than was expected.	

Total Score _____

Ready-to-Use Independent Reading Management Kit: Grades 4–6 Scholastic Professional Books

Student's Name _____ Date _____

Independent Reading Contract _____

Book Title _____

Assessment Rubric

	1 Point	2 Points	3 Points	Score
Reading				
BOOK SELECTION	Book matched neither reading level nor interest.	Book matched either reading level or interest.	Book matched both reading level and interest.	
FLUENCY/ EXPRESSION	Student read some parts with fluency and expression.	Student read most parts with fluency and expression.	Student read all parts with fluency and expression.	
COMPRE-HENSION	Student demonstrated understanding of some of the text.	Student demonstrated understanding of most of the text.	Student demonstrated understanding of all of the text.	
Writing				
PRESENTATION	Some of student's work is neat and organized.	Most of student's work is neat and organized.	All of student's work is neat and organized.	
QUALITY OF WORK	Some of student's work shows thoughtfulness and understanding.	Most of student's work shows thoughtfulness and understanding.	All of student's work shows thoughtfulness and understanding.	
EFFICIENCY	Student took longer than expected to complete work.	Student completed work on time.	Student completed work sooner than was expected.	
Skills				
PRESENTATION	Some of student's work is neat and organized.	Most of student's work is neat and organized.	All of student's work is neat and organized.	
QUALITY OF WORK	Some of student's work shows thoughtfulness and understanding.	Most of student's work shows thoughtfulness and understanding.	All of student's work shows thoughtfulness and understanding.	
EFFICIENCY	Student took longer than expected to complete work.	Student completed work on time.	Student completed work sooner than was expected.	
Art				
PRESENTATION	Some of student's work is neat and organized.	Most of student's work is neat and organized.	All of student's work is neat and organized.	
QUALITY OF WORK	Some of student's work shows thoughtfulness and understanding.	Most of student's work shows thoughtfulness and understanding.	All of student's work shows thoughtfulness and understanding.	
EFFICIENCY	Student took longer than expected to complete work.	Student completed work on time.	Student completed work sooner than was expected.	

Total Score _____

Comments: _____

_____

_____

Teacher Record

Student _____

Independent Reading Contract _____ Date _____

Book Title and Author: _____

_____

Self-Assessment Rubric Score: _____

Assessment Rubric Score: _____

Comments: _____

_____

Independent Reading Contract _____ Date _____

Book Title and Author: _____

_____

Self-Assessment Rubric Score: _____

Assessment Rubric Score: _____

Comments: _____

_____

Independent Reading Contract _____ Date _____

Book Title and Author: _____

_____

Self-Assessment Rubric Score: _____

Assessment Rubric Score: _____

Comments: _____

_____

Ready-to-Use Independent Reading Management Kit: Grades 4–6   Scholastic Professional Books

Dear _____,

Throughout the year, students in my class will be reading books of their choice. To help children get the most out of their books, our reading program features independent reading contracts. Each contract offers a variety of activities that encourage students to respond to literature in meaningful ways. The activities include reading comprehension, writing, vocabulary, grammar, spelling, art, and more. Each contract is designed for a specific genre: fiction, biography, mystery, realistic fiction, adventure, and nonfiction. Children are encouraged to complete contracts for books in each genre.

In addition to building important language-arts skills, independent reading contracts help students learn to work independently and purposefully. Although the contracts feature a wide variety of activities, the structure and procedures are consistent. This allows children to work on their own while I meet with individuals or small groups of students. When they have finished a contract, children will meet with me to talk about the book they read and the activities they completed.

The goal of our independent reading program is to foster a love of reading and to help children build important reading and writing skills. I look forward to helping each student reach this goal. Please feel free to call me if you have questions.

Sincerely,

_____

Independent Reading Contract

Book Title _____

This book was: (easy) **1** **2** **3** **4** **5** (difficult)

Complete the activities based on your independent reading book.
When you have finished an activity, check the box.

Reading	Writing	Skills	Art
(Choose _____)	**(Choose _____)**	**(Choose _____)**	**(Choose _____)**

Ready-to-Use Independent Reading Management Kit: Grades 4–6 Scholastic Professional Books

Notes

Notes